Maps and Mapping

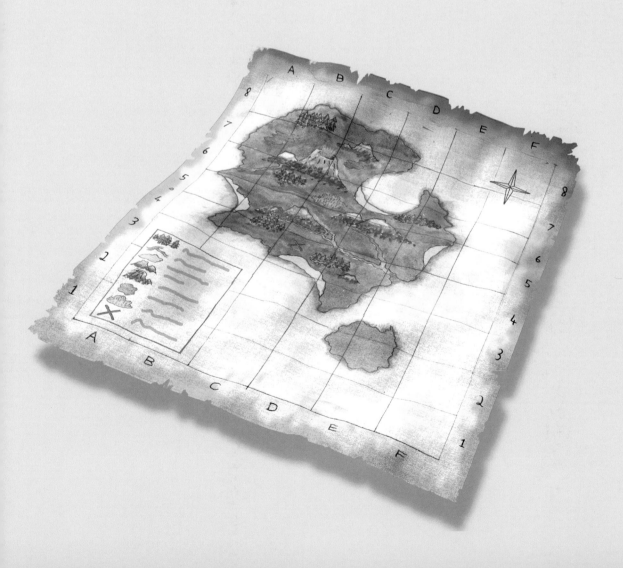

KINGFISHER

LONDON & NEW YORK

Copyright © Kingfisher 2010
Published in the United States by Kingfisher,
175 Fifth Ave., New York, NY 10010
Kingfisher is an imprint of Macmillan Children's Books, London.
All rights reserved.

First published as *Kingfisher Young Knowledge: Maps and Mapping* in 2004
Additional material produced for Kingfisher by Discovery Books Ltd.

Distributed in the U.S. by Macmillan, 175 Fifth Ave., New York, NY 10010
Distributed in Canada by H.B. Fenn and Company Ltd.,
34 Nixon Road, Bolton, Ontario L7E 1W2

Library of Congress Cataloging-in-Publication data has been applied for.

ISBN: 978-0-7534-6450-2

Kingfisher books are available for special promotions and premiums.
For details contact: Special Markets Department, Macmillan,
175 Fifth Avenue, New York, NY 10010.

For more information, please visit www.kingfisherbooks.com

Printed in China
10 9 8 7 6 5 4 3 2 1
1TR/0410/WKT/UNTD/140MA/C

Note to readers: the website addresses listed in this book are correct at
the time of going to print. However, due to the ever-changing nature
of the Internet, website addresses and content can change. Websites
can contain links that are unsuitable for children. The publisher cannot
be held responsible for changes in website addresses or content or
for information obtained through a third party. We strongly advise
that Internet searches be supervised by an adult.

Acknowledgments
The publishers would like to thank the following for permission to reproduce their material. Every care has been taken
to trace copyright holders. However, if there have been unintentional omissions or failure to trace copyright holders,
we apologize and will, if informed, endeavor to make corrections in any future edition.
b = bottom, *c* = center, *l* = left, *t* = top, *r* = right

Cover main Shutterstock/Parfta; cover *l* Shutterstock/Bonsai; cover *r* Shutterstock/Haider: 2–3 British Library; 4–5 British Library; 8–9 Corbis;
12 Corbis; 14–15*t* Zefa; 14–15*b* Corbis; 16 Portuguese Tourist Office; 17 Alamy; 18–19 Getty Images; 19*tl* Frank Lane Picture Agency; 19*br* Frank
Lane Picture Agency; 20–21 Corbis; 26 Hereford Cathedral; 27 Getty Images; 28 Corbis; 29*t* Science Photo Library; 29*b* NASA; 30–31 Science
Photo Library; 33*t* Heritage Image Partnership; 33*b* Corbis; 34–35 Science Photo Library; 36 Corbis; 36–37 Science Photo Library; 38–39*t* Zefa;
38–39*b* Science Photo Library; 40 Art Archive; 40–41 Science Photo Library; 41 NASA; 48*t* Shutterstock Images/Sandra van der Steen;
48*b* Shutterstock Images; 49*t* Shutterstock Images/sizov; 49*b* Shutterstock Images/vrihu; 52 Shutterstock Images/7505811966;
53*t* Shutterstock Images/IgorXIII; 53*b* Shutterstock Images/HomeStudio; 56 Shutterstock Images/Henrik Lehnerer

Commissioned photography on pages 42–47 by Andy Crawford
Thank you to models Lewis Manu and Rebecca Roper

Maps and Mapping

Deborah Chancellor

KINGFISHER

NEW YORK

Contents

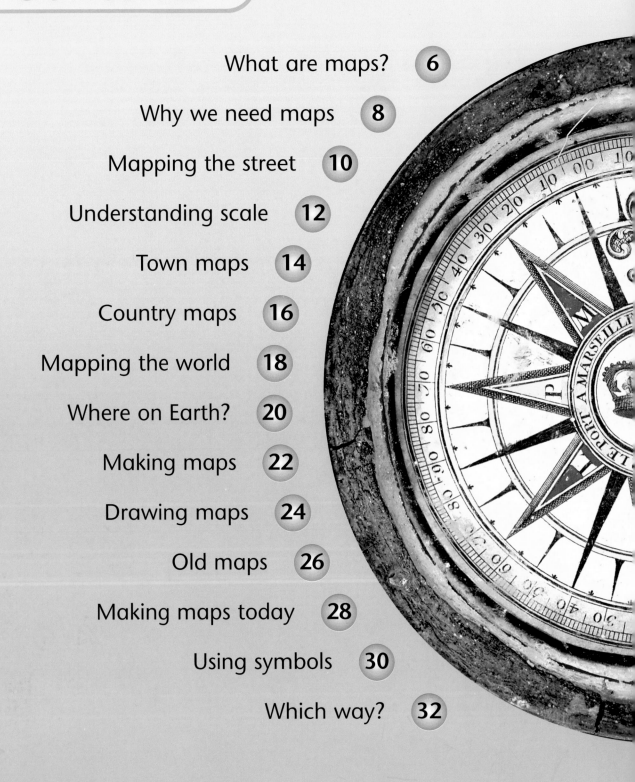

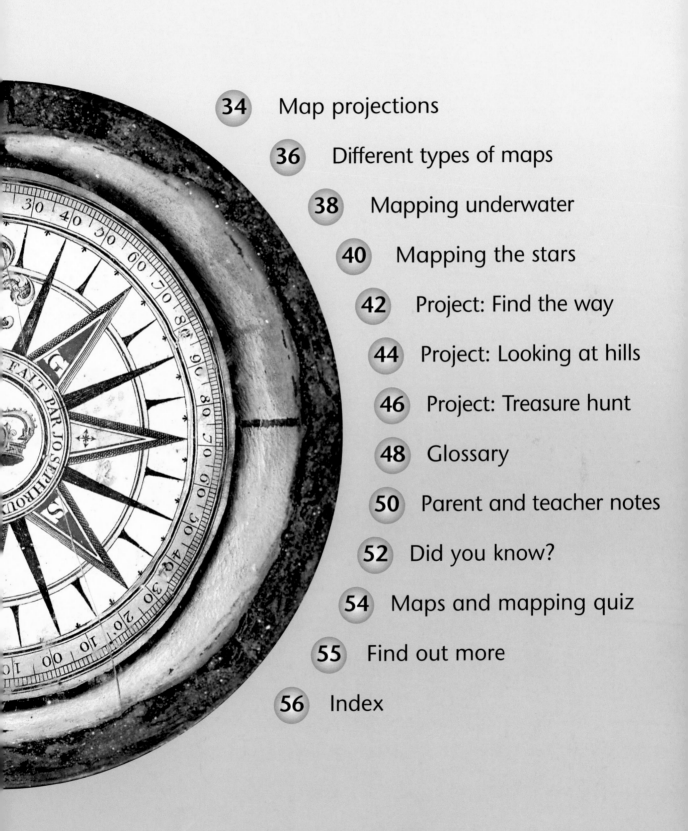

What are maps?

Maps show us what places look like from above. Some maps cover small areas. Others show big countries— or even the whole world.

Learning from maps

Maps give us useful information about countries. This map of Australia shows the main cities, roads, and rivers.

Finding places

Maps show us where we are. Grids are put on top of maps to help us find different places.

How far?

Scale bars on maps show how many miles per inch (or kilometers per centimeter) there are. You can then measure distances on the map.

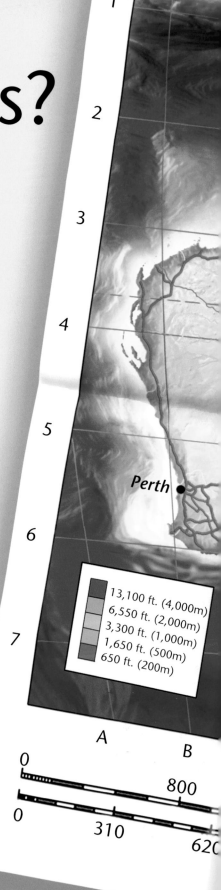

1
2
3
4
5
6
7

Perth

13,100 ft. (4,000m)
6,550 ft. (2,000m)
3,300 ft. (1,000m)
1,650 ft. (500m)
650 ft. (200m)

A
B

0
800
0
310
620

7

Darwin

Broome

Cairns

Townsville

Alice Springs

Brisbane

Adelaide

Sydney

Canberra

Melbourne

■ Capital city
● City or town
〜 Major road
〜 River

Hobart

C   D   E   F   G   H   I   J

1,600 kilometers

930 miles

Why we need maps

Maps teach us about places. You can spot where countries and continents are on a world map. Important cities are marked with dots, and lines show where borders are.

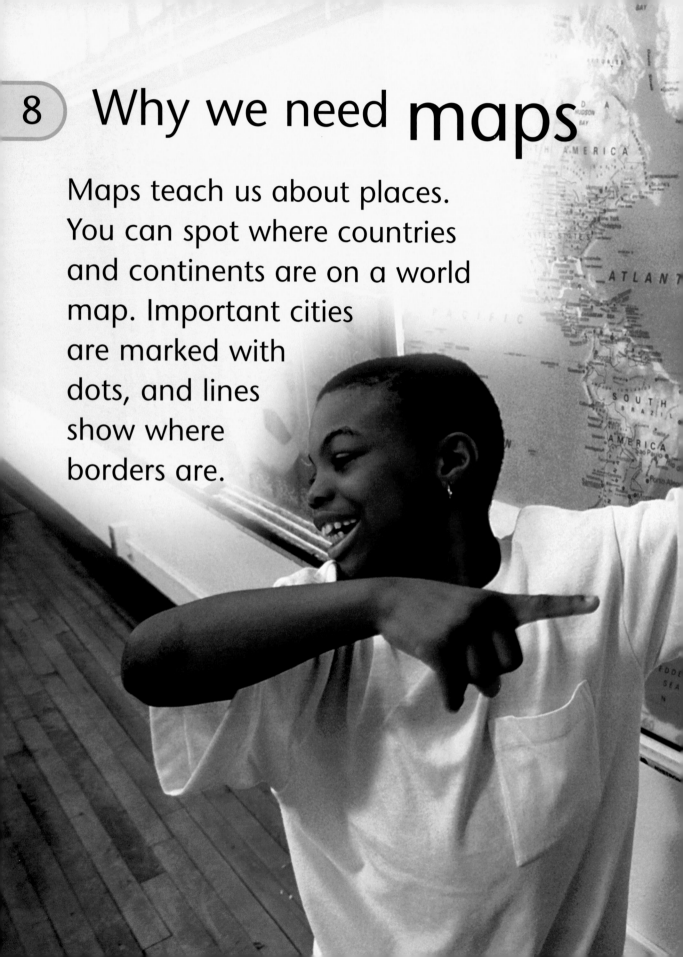

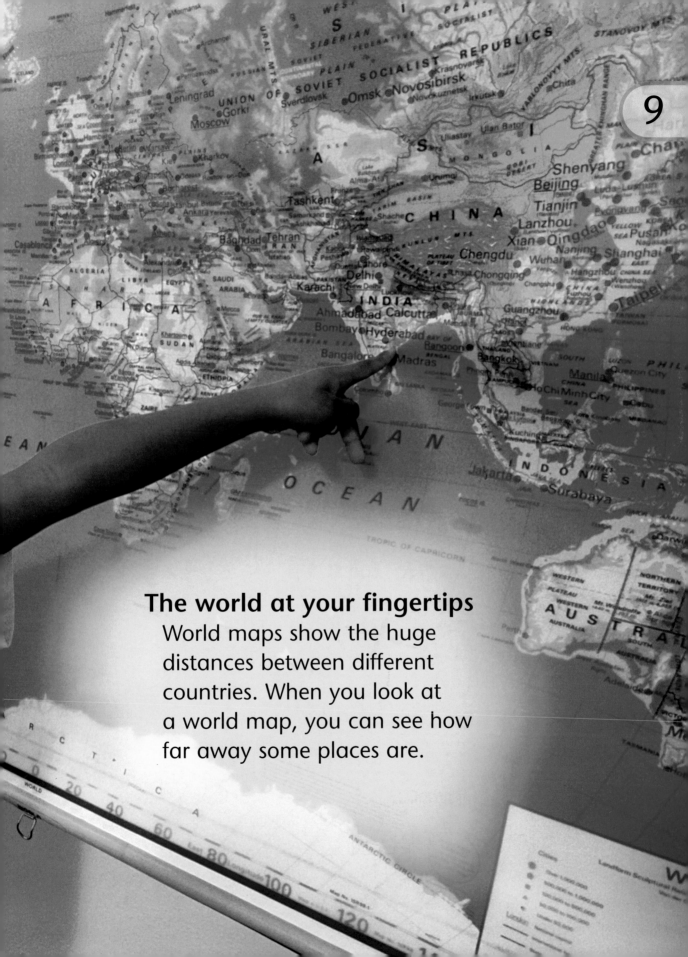

The world at your fingertips
World maps show the huge
distances between different
countries. When you look at
a world map, you can see how
far away some places are.

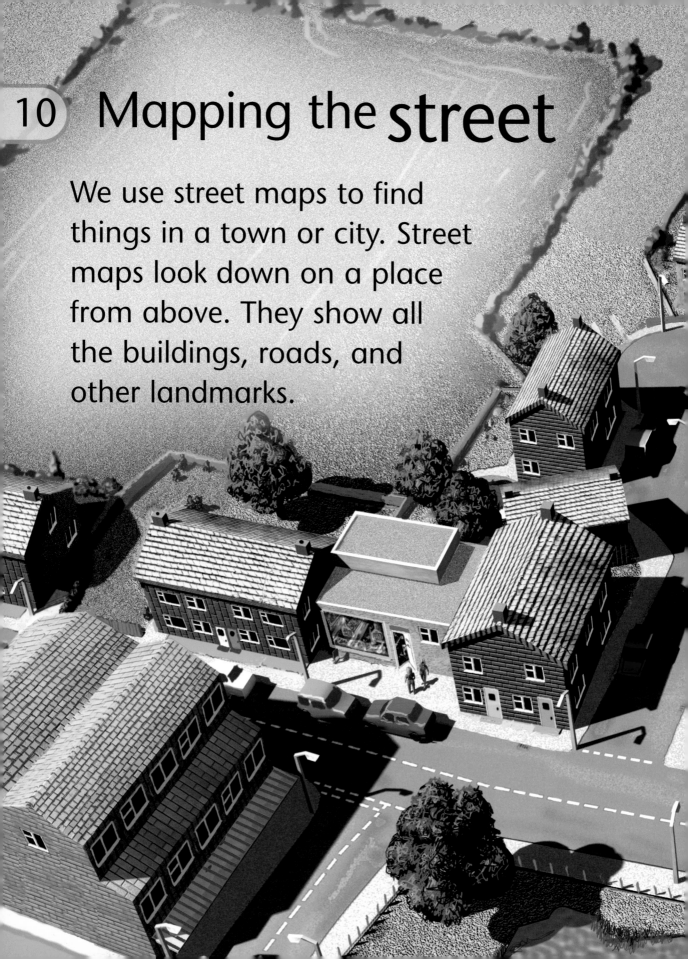

Mapping the street

We use street maps to find things in a town or city. Street maps look down on a place from above. They show all the buildings, roads, and other landmarks.

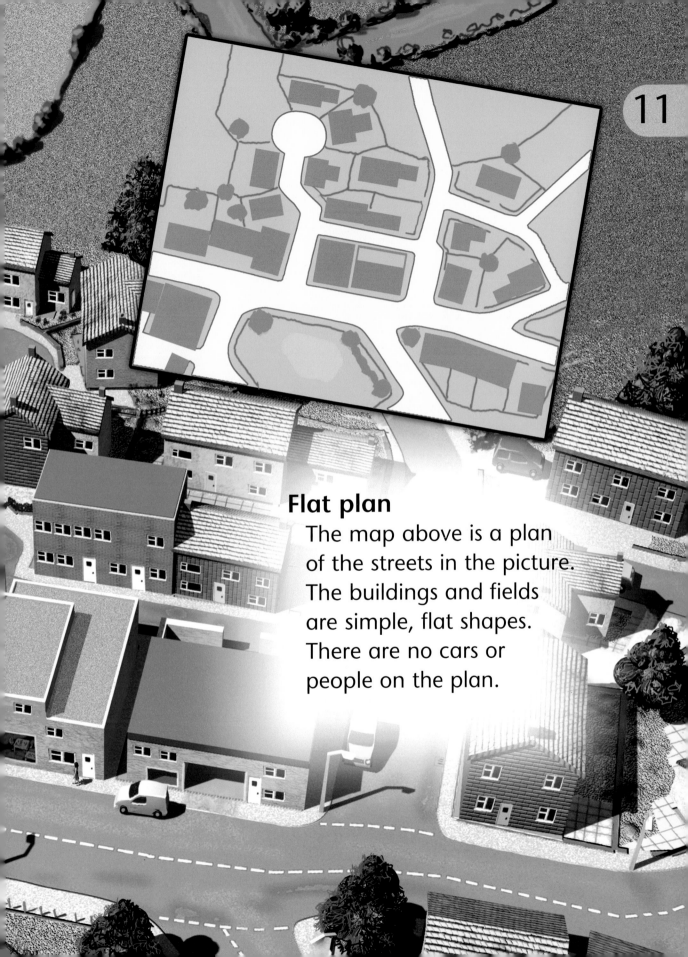

Flat plan

The map above is a plan of the streets in the picture. The buildings and fields are simple, flat shapes. There are no cars or people on the plan.

Understanding scale

Small-scale maps
show big areas
of land and water.
Large-scale maps
show much smaller
areas in a lot
more detail.

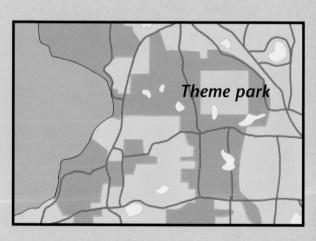

Theme park map
This map has a large scale.
It gives a lot of detail.

Shrink to fit

Everything on a map has
to be shrunk to fit. Small-
scale maps shrink things
even more than large-scale
maps so that they can
show a bigger area.

Theme park

Road map
This road map has a smaller
scale. It shows where to find
the theme park.

13

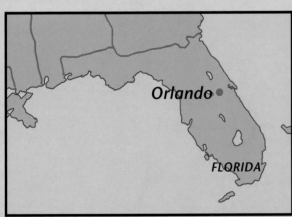

State map

The theme park is in Orlando. This city is just a dot on a Florida state map.

Country map

This map shows the United States. It has the smallest scale on this page.

Town maps

We need several different types of maps in a town or city. If we are walking or driving, street maps are very useful. Bus or train maps help us plan our trips on public transportation.

Finding your way

Tourist maps are sometimes done in 3-D. They illustrate the landmarks in a city. The red line on this map shows the route a tourist has planned to find his way around.

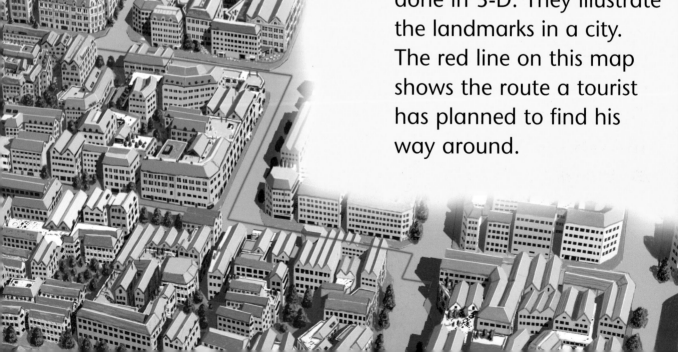

Street-smart

Buildings and roads look very small on maps, but they are much bigger in real life. This busy street in Paris would look very different on a street map.

Train map

On maps of the subway in Paris, France, train routes are shown with lines. Each route has its own color and number. The names of all the stations are marked on the map.

16 Country maps

Maps of countries cover large areas. They show important features such as mountains, cities, and borders. Symbols on country maps show points of interest.

Capital city

The dots on this map represent capital cities. Lisbon is the capital of Portugal. It was built around a natural harbor.

PORTUGAL

Lisbon

Natural border

These mountains form a natural border between Spain and France. They are in a mountain range called the Pyrenees.

FRANCE

Borders between countries are marked with a red line.

Pyrenees

SPAIN

● **Madrid**

 Flamenco dancing

 Fishing

 Winemaking

 Orange growing

 Watersports

 Tourist area

Mapping the world

World maps are covered with a grid of lines. These are called lines of latitude and longitude. We use them to figure out the exact positions of places.

Starting at Greenwich

The prime meridian is the line of longitude that passes through Greenwich, England. It marks 0° (degrees) longitude. All other lines of longitude are measured east or west of this line.

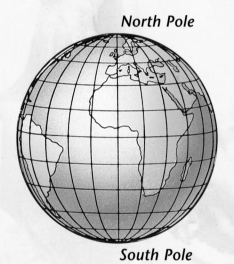

North Pole

South Pole

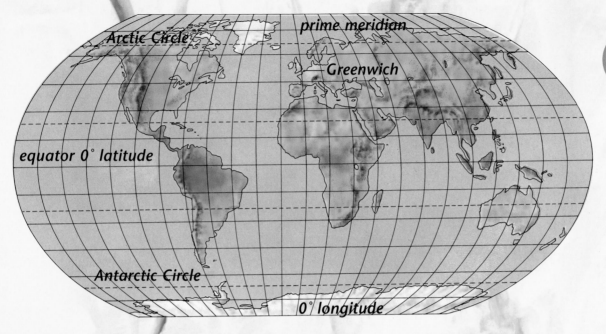

prime meridian

Arctic Circle

Greenwich

equator 0° latitude

Antarctic Circle

0° longitude

At the poles

All lines of longitude meet at the North and South poles. These penguins live in Antarctica—the frozen continent around the South Pole in the Antarctic Circle.

In the middle

The equator is an imaginary line that runs around the middle of Earth. All lines of latitude are measured north or south of the equator.

Where on Earth?

Any position on Earth can be described with measurements of latitude and longitude. Grids on maps help us find a particular place—such as a city on a world map or buried gold on a treasure map.

Global address

A city's position of latitude and longitude is like an "address" on a world map. New Orleans, Louisiana, is 30° north and 90° west.

Out to sea

The Mississippi River flows through New Orleans and out into the Gulf of Mexico. This busy route for river traffic is 2,300 miles (3,700 kilometers) long.

Finding hiding places

Even treasure maps have grids marked on them. Any place or thing on the map can be given a grid reference using letters and numbers at the edge of the grid.

A B C D

8

7

6

5

4

3

Forest
River
Beach
Mountain
Volcano
Lake
Swamp
Treasure

N
W   E
S

B

C

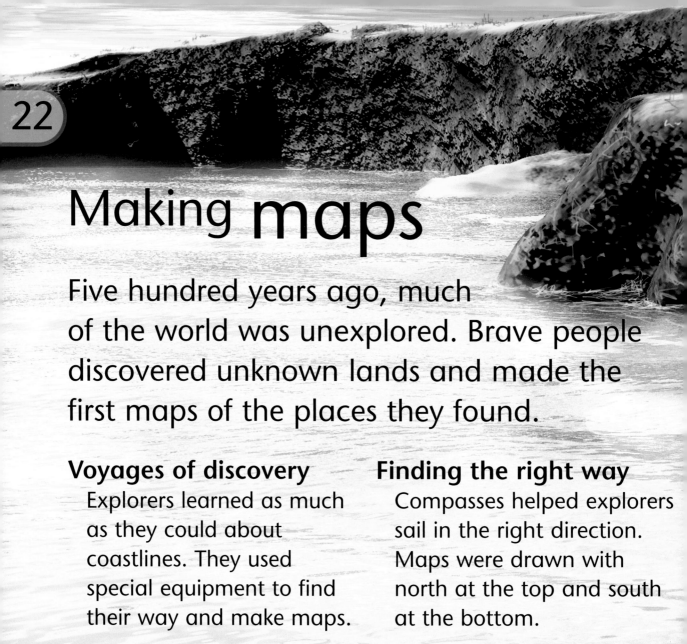

Making maps

Five hundred years ago, much of the world was unexplored. Brave people discovered unknown lands and made the first maps of the places they found.

Voyages of discovery

Explorers learned as much as they could about coastlines. They used special equipment to find their way and make maps.

Finding the right way

Compasses helped explorers sail in the right direction. Maps were drawn with north at the top and south at the bottom.

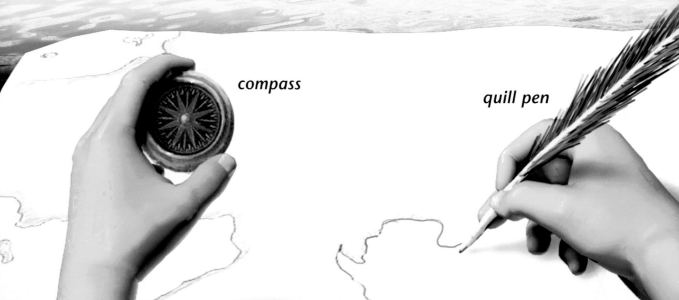

compass

quill pen

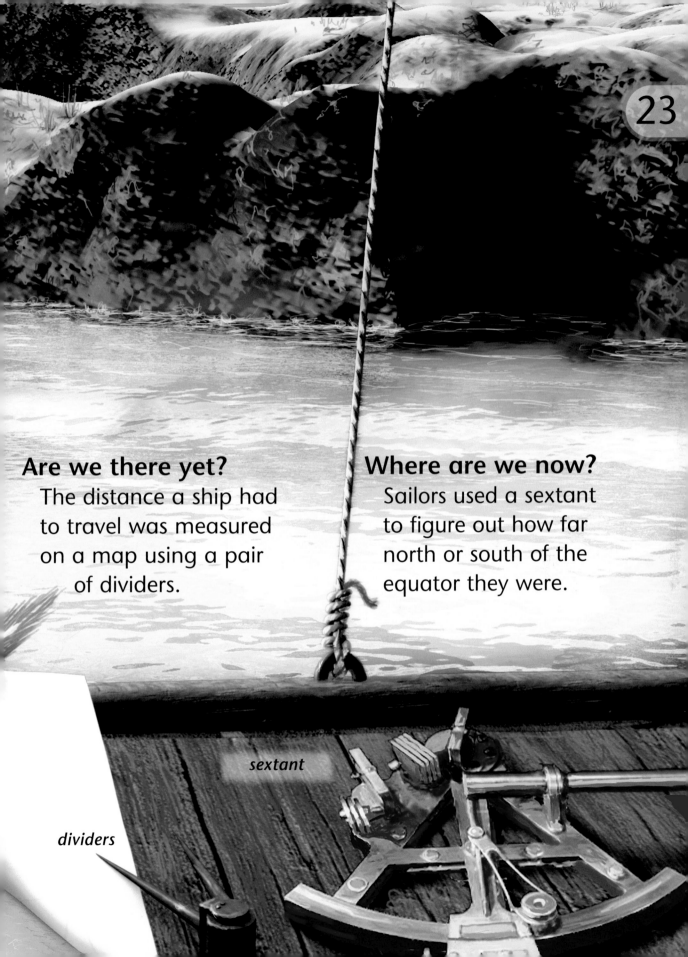

Are we there yet?

The distance a ship had to travel was measured on a map using a pair of dividers.

Where are we now?

Sailors used a sextant to figure out how far north or south of the equator they were.

sextant

dividers

Drawing maps

You need a lot of information about the landscape in order to draw an exact and correct map. Many measurements must be taken, such as the heights of mountains and the lengths of rivers.

Surveying the land

Surveyors are people who measure features of the landscape so that maps can be made. They record every detail—for example, whether it is woody or bare, dry or swampy.

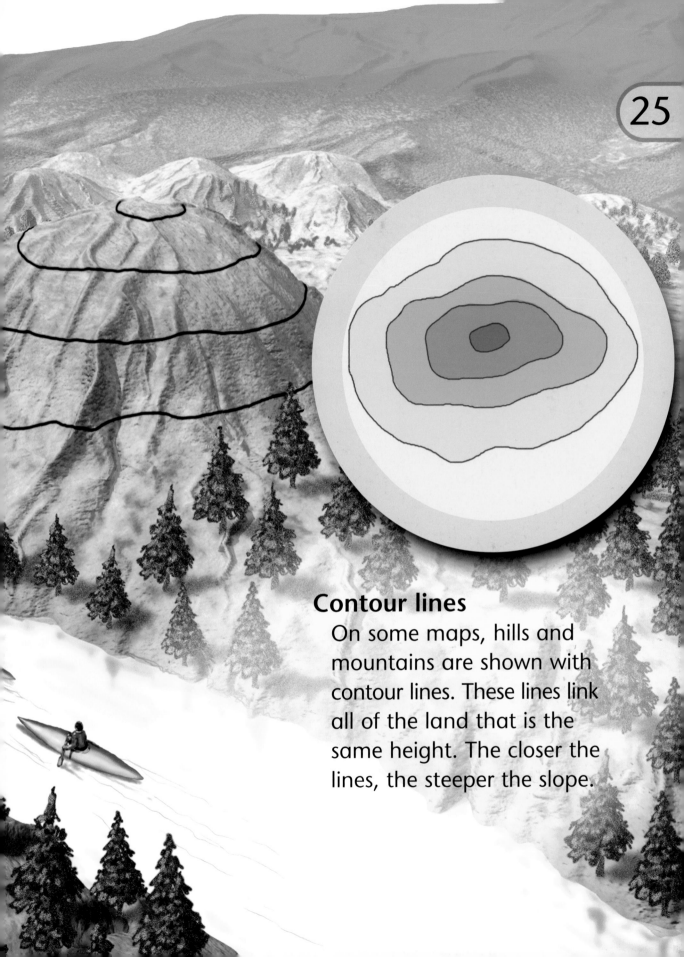

Contour lines

On some maps, hills and
mountains are shown with
contour lines. These lines link
all of the land that is the
same height. The closer the
lines, the steeper the slope.

Old maps

People have been making maps for thousands of years. The first maps of the whole world were made about 1,800 years ago. They show only the countries and oceans that people knew about at the time.

What's missing?

The first mapmakers did not know that the Americas, Australia, and Antarctica existed. This map shows what some people thought the world looked like about 900 years ago.

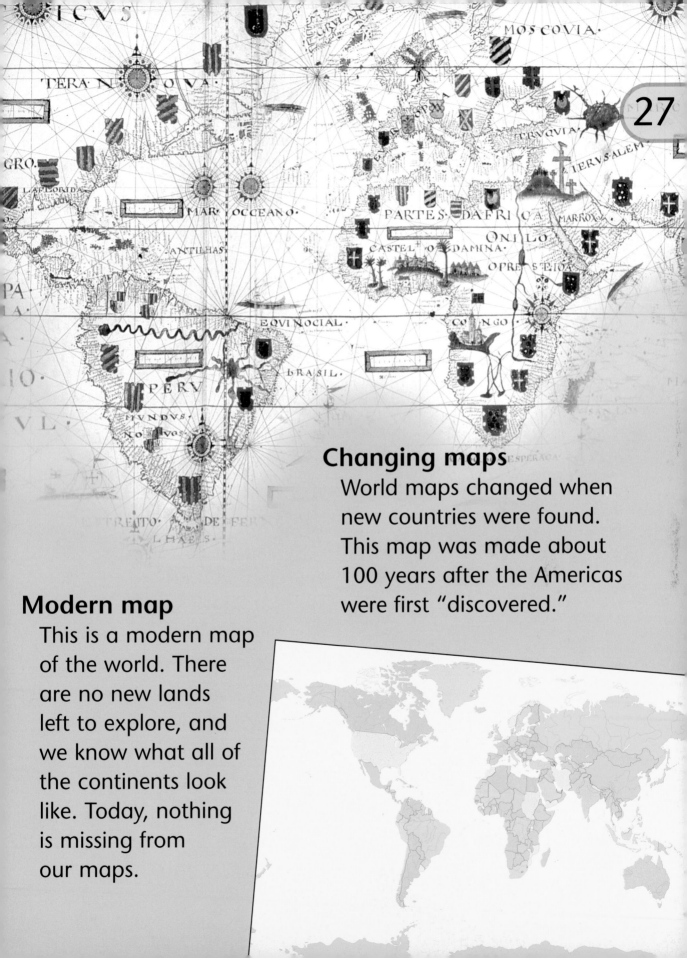

Changing maps

World maps changed when new countries were found. This map was made about 100 years after the Americas were first "discovered."

Modern map

This is a modern map of the world. There are no new lands left to explore, and we know what all of the continents look like. Today, nothing is missing from our maps.

Making maps today

New technology helps us make maps. Photographs of land and water can be taken from aircraft and satellites. Cartographers use these images along with other information to create maps.

Using computers

Today, cartographers use computers to help them make maps. A lot of geographical data can be stored on a computer database and used to create many different types of maps. This is a digital map of part of Asia.

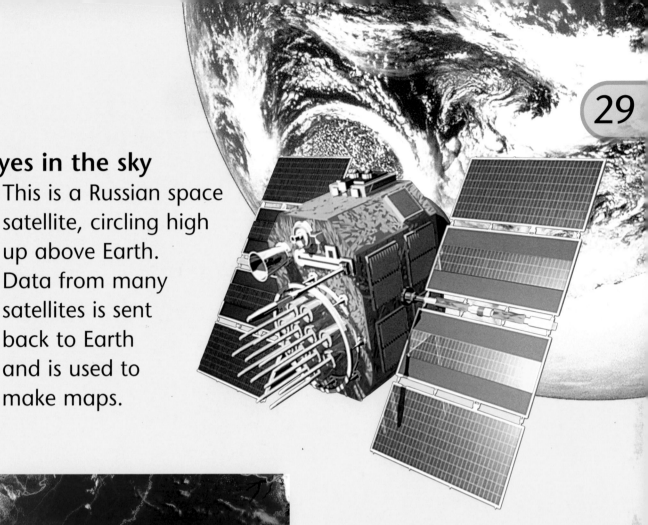

Eyes in the sky

This is a Russian space satellite, circling high up above Earth. Data from many satellites is sent back to Earth and is used to make maps.

Looking down

The Amazon River in northern Brazil looks like this from space. The dark areas are rainforest, and the river is a thin yellow line. Satellite photos give cartographers a detailed picture of the landscape.

30 Using symbols

Maps need to crowd a lot of information into a small space. Symbols and colors on maps are used to show many different things on the ground.

Flying over London

This is a bird's-eye view of central London, England. Street maps of the area show all the roads, buildings, and parks. Symbols tell us what important buildings are used for.

Map key

Symbols and colors on a map are explained in a key. We need to look at the key to understand what the map is showing us.

P	Parking lot
i	Information
⊖	Subway
▭	Police station
+	Hospital
	Park
	Housing area
	Business area
✡	Synagogue
☾	Mosque
✝	Church

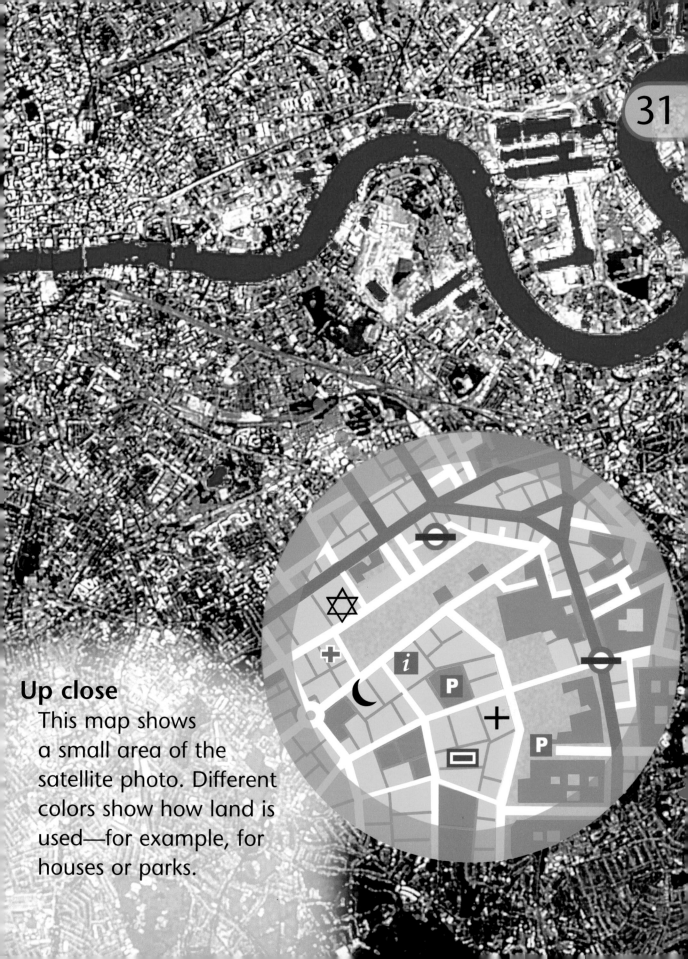

Up close
This map shows a small area of the satellite photo. Different colors show how land is used—for example, for houses or parks.

Which way?

Whichever way you look, you are facing a particular direction. This will be somewhere between north, south, east, and west. You can use a compass to find your direction.

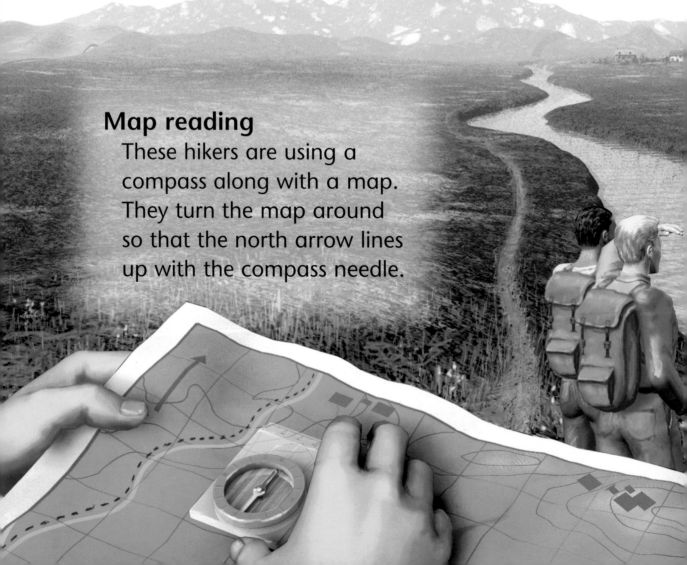

Map reading
These hikers are using a compass along with a map. They turn the map around so that the north arrow lines up with the compass needle.

Map projections

The most accurate world maps are globes because they show the land and water as they really are. Flat maps change the shape of some countries.

Projections

The way we show the curved Earth on a flat map is called a projection. The projection on the right is a "Mercator" projection.

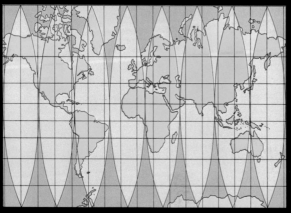

Flat map

A globe can be split into segments and "peeled" like an orange. The segments are placed side by side to make a flat map that looks like this.

Different views

There are many different map
projections. The one below
splits the globe up in a special
way so that countries and
oceans are not too distorted.

Different types of maps

There are many types of maps. Maps can give information about things such as the weather. They can also show how places compare with one another.

Underwater maps

Maps of the oceans and seas are called charts. They help boats follow routes and avoid danger. The crosses on this chart stand for shipwrecks on the seabed.

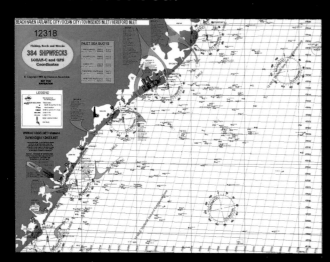

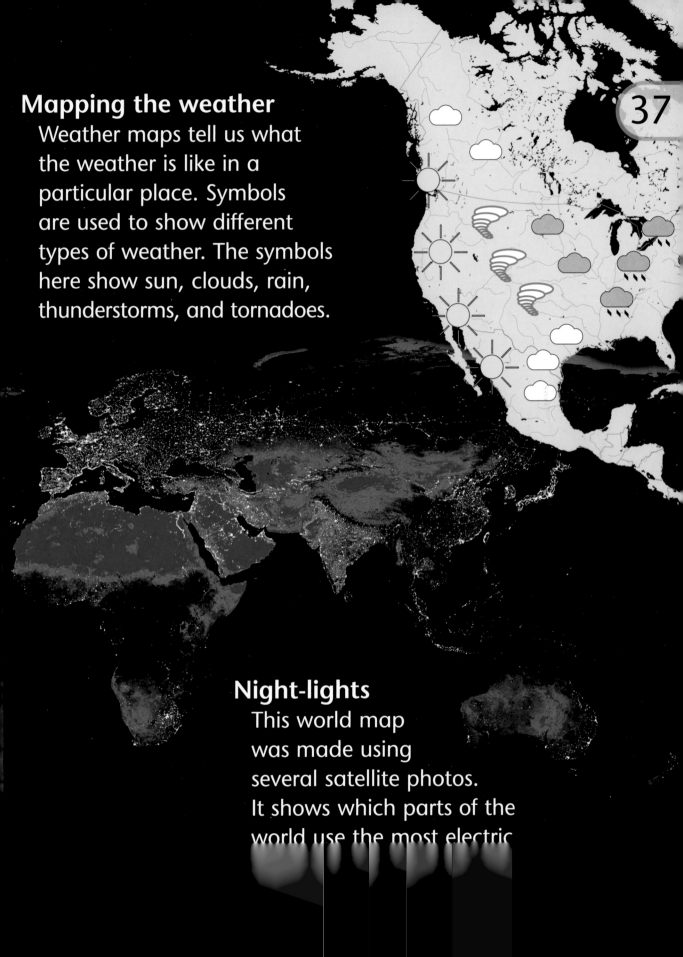

Mapping the weather

Weather maps tell us what
the weather is like in a
particular place. Symbols
are used to show different
types of weather. The symbols
here show sun, clouds, rain,
thunderstorms, and tornadoes.

Night-lights

This world map
was made using
several satellite photos.
It shows which parts of the
world use the most electric

Mapping underwater

There are huge mountains and deep canyons under the sea. Measurements of these features are taken so that maps showing the seabed can be made.

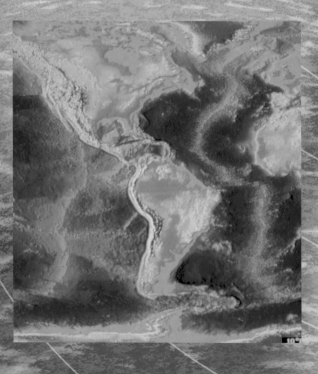

Ocean ridges

Underwater mountain ranges are called ocean ridges. They can be very long. On this map, the deepest water is dark blue. The ocean ridges are the lightest blue.

Deep blue sea

Special equipment measures how long sound takes to reach the seabed and bounce back again. The depth of the water can then be figured out.

Diving for data

Deep-sea submersibles are small submarines that take divers down to explore the seabed. Measurements are taken by divers to provide data for maps.

Mapping the stars

People who study the stars in the sky are called astronomers. Today's astronomers look at distant galaxies through powerful telescopes. Then they make space maps called star charts.

Seeing stars

You can look at the stars using a regular pair of binoculars. Some constellations can be seen from the northern half of the world, while others can be seen from the south.

Star charts

Long ago, people named
constellations after
animals, heroes, and gods.
They painted beautiful
charts to show the positions
of the stars in the sky.

Mapping the Moon

Maps are also made of the
Moon. Photographs are
used to make maps of
the craters, valleys, and
canyons on the surface
of the Moon.

Find the way

Make your own compass

A compass needle is a magnet that points north. You can turn a needle into a magnet and then float it in water to make a compass.

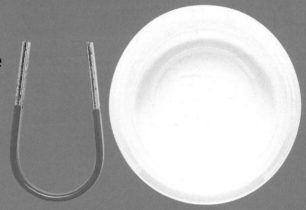

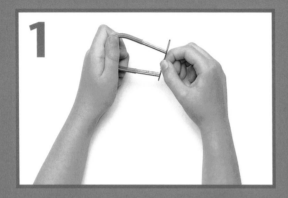

1

Hold the needle and gently rub it with the magnet. Do this about 50 times, always rubbing in the same direction.

You will need:
- Large needle
- Magnet
- Cork
- Tub of water
- Compass

2

Ask an adult to cut a slice of cork for you. Carefully balance the needle on top of the cork and float it in a tub of water.

3

Place a compass next to your floating needle. Both "compass needles" should be facing the same direction—north!

Mapping your bedroom

You can draw a map of your bedroom using your footsteps to measure what is there. Count how many footsteps it takes to walk the length and width of your room. You will need some paper, a ruler, and some markers or pens to make your map.

Draw an outline of your bedroom. Fill it in with a grid. Each square on the grid stands for one footstep.

Measure your furniture in footsteps. Draw furniture shapes on your map, putting them in the right places.

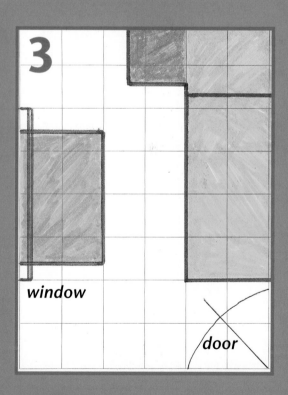

window

door

Add the door and any windows. Color in all of the furniture using markers or pens. You can draw a map key to explain your colors.

Looking at hills

Make a relief map

Some maps use color shading and modeling to show how land varies in height. Mountains and valleys are easy to see on a relief map. You can make a relief map using craft materials.

Roll up three balls of newspaper. Make each ball a different size. Firmly stick the balls to the thick cardboard using tape.

You will need:
- Newspaper
- Piece of thick cardboard
- Tape
- Scissors
- Glue or flour-and-water paste
- Paper towels
- Poster paints
- Paintbrush

Cut some pieces of newspaper into thin strips. Glue the strips over the newspaper balls. Add several layers and then leave them to dry.

3

Glue a layer of paper towels over the map. Remember to cover the cardboard base as well as the "hills." Leave everything to dry.

4

Paint your map with bands of color. Use different colors to show different heights. Land of the same height should be the same color.

On this map, green shows low ground. Yellow shades stand for medium height, and dark brown means higher ground.

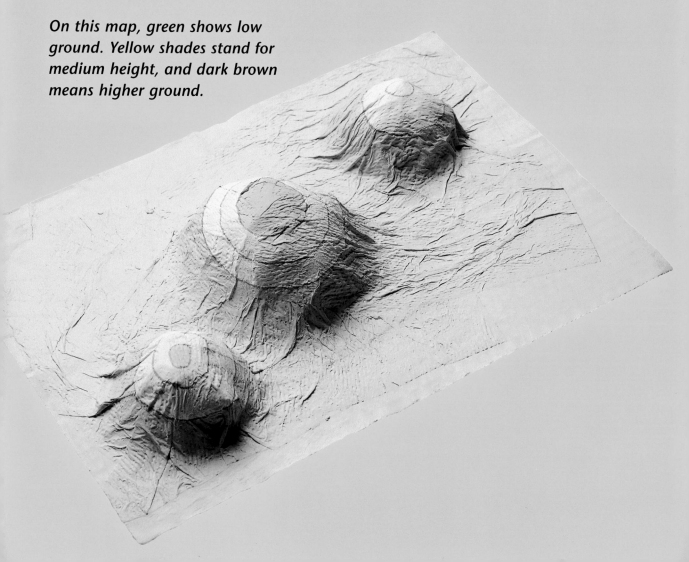

Treasure hunt

Make a treasure map

In stories, old maps of desert islands help people find buried treasure. Make your own treasure map for a make-believe island.

Scrunch up a piece of paper into a loose ball. Flatten it out again with your hands.

You will need:
- Paper
- Poster paints
- Paintbrush
- Pencil
- Ruler
- Markers
- Scissors

Dilute some green or brown paint to make it very watery. Paint this over the whole sheet of crumpled paper. Leave it to dry.

Draw a grid of squares over the paper with a pencil and a ruler. Each line should be the same distance apart.

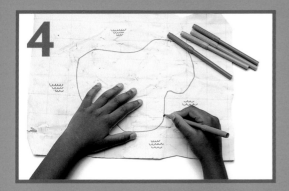

Draw the outline of a desert island. Make it an interesting, unusual shape. Add some waves to show where the water is.

Draw some pictures on your map to stand for different things such as lakes or volcanoes. Make the symbols small and simple.

Ask your friends to figure out where the treasure is buried.

Draw a key to explain your symbols and add a north arrow. Shade the edges to make the map look old.

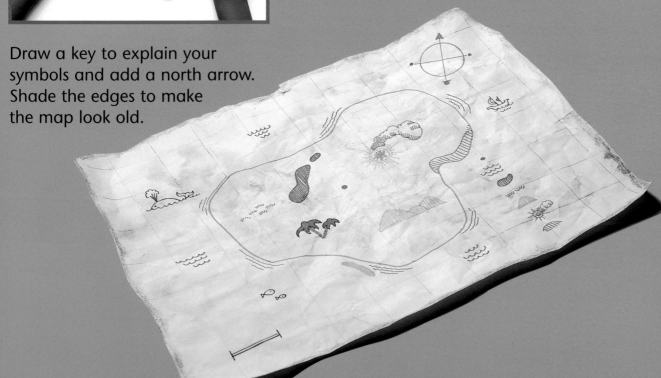

Glossary

3-D—three-dimensional. It means showing several different sides of an object so that it does not look flat.

bird's-eye view—the way something looks from directly above, as though you were a bird flying overhead

border—a place where one country or state meets another country or state

canyon—a deep valley with very steep sides

capital city—the large city where a country's government meets

cartographer—a person who makes maps

chart—a map of the sea, sky, or space

compass—a device that uses magnetism to show which way is north from anywhere in the world

constellation—a group of several stars that make up a shape that is visible from Earth

continent—an enormous area of land such as North America, Europe, or Africa

data—scientific information that comes from experiments, research, or measurements

database—an organized file of information that can be stored on a computer

digital—a type of information that is stored and viewed on a computer

distorted—changed from the usual shape

dividers—instruments used for measuring and dividing lines on a map

galaxy—a very large group of stars and planets

geographical data—information about Earth's features

globe—a ball with a map of the world on it

grid—a pattern of lines that cross one another

grid reference—on a map, letters or numbers along the edges of the grid that indicate one of the squares on the grid

landmark—a recognizable or large feature of a place

latitude—how far a point is north or south of the equator

longitude—how far a point is east or west of the prime meridian

natural border—a place where two countries meet at a natural dividing feature such as a river or a mountain range

natural harbor—a place where the landscape has naturally formed an enclosed area of water. Natural harbors are often found where a river joins the ocean or sea.

position—the exact place where something is

projection—in mapping, a way of making a map of the round Earth fit onto a flat map

relief map—a type of map that uses colors to show the heights of different areas

ridge—a range of mountains

sextant—a device for figuring out latitude

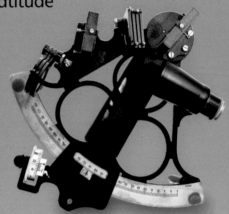

state—some countries, such as the U.S., are divided into areas called states. Sometimes *state* can also mean a whole country.

submarine—a machine that can travel underwater. Many submarines can carry people.

surveyor—a person who measures different features of a landscape. This information allows maps to be made.

telescope—a device used for making things that are very far away appear bigger

This book will be useful in teaching and reinforcing different aspects of the language arts and geography curricula in the elementary grades. It also provides opportunities for crosscurricular activities in science, math, technology, and art.

Extension activities

Language arts
Writing
1) Create an exciting pirate adventure story to go with the treasure map on page 21, or your project on pages 46–47. Include how the pirates got the treasure and why they buried it.

2) You are piloting a submersible (pp. 38–39) on an area of seabed that has never before been mapped or observed up close. Write a log describing your observations and discoveries. Include a map showing your route and points of interest.

Speaking and listening
1) Research a country that is of interest to you. Draw a map similar to the one on pages 16–17 showing key locations and points of interest. Give a short oral report on your country using your map as a visual aid.

2) Hide some treasure (a penny will do) in an open area such as a neighborhood park. Make a treasure map with lots of twists and turns leading from a starting point to the treasure. Use your map to guide a friend along the path using only spoken directions.

Geography
The topic of mapping relates to the themes of chronological and spatial thinking, as well as using map skills to determine locations and interpret information through legend, scale, and symbols. Some specific links include identifying and using map symbols (pp. 6, 30–31); constructing maps and models (pp. 10–11, 24–25, 28–29, 34–41, 43–47); distance and scale (pp. 6–7, 12–13); latitude and longitude (pp. 18–21); historical significance (pp. 22–23, 26–27, 41); and using maps to display specific information such as routes,

physical features, weather, and so forth (pp. 8–9, 14–17, 24–25, 36–41).

Crosscurricular links
1) Science: Specific links to science curricula include the use of maps to locate stars and planets (pp. 40–41) and geological features (pp. 36–39) and to interpret and predict weather (p. 37).

2) Math: Use a map with a mileage key to determine the distance between different locations. Make up problems using this information.

3) Technology: Go to *www.infoplease.com/atlas/ latitude-longitude.html* and find out your town or city's latitude and longitude. Copy the numbers into the search box at *http://maps.google.com.* Use the tabs and zoom function to view the region in different map formats and scales.

4) Art: Make drawings of several constellations. Find out how each got its name and put all the information together in a booklet.

Using the projects
Children can do these projects at home. Here are some ideas for extending them:

Page 42: Plot a route around your school or neighborhood with a real compass, using paces and compass directions. Ask a friend to try your compass trek.

Page 43: Make a second map of your bedroom using your own body length as the unit of measurement. You might have to round your measurements to the nearest whole number. How do the maps compare? Which is more accurate?

Page 44–45: Cover one of your hills with clear plastic wrap. Pull it down tight and tape it lightly in place. Use a permanent marker to trace the bands showing different heights. Carefully undo the tape and spread out the plastic wrap. You will have a flat contour map.

Did you know?

- One of the oldest maps of the world that you can still see is the Babylonian world map. It was made of clay in about 600 B.C. It is now displayed at the British Museum in London, England.

- In 1154, Arab geographer Muhammad al-Idrisi made an atlas called the *Tabula Rogeriana*. It showed almost all of Europe and Asia, as well as North Africa. No one made a more accurate map for 300 years!

- The British mapmaking agency Ordnance Survey started work on its first map in 1795. It took six years to make! The map showed the county of Kent in southeast England.

- There are parts of the Moon's surface that have been more fully explored than some parts of the Amazon rainforest here on Earth.

- The Northern Hemisphere is the same size as the Southern Hemisphere, but it contains about 90 percent of the world's population.

- Town maps might seem modern, but the Romans had a map of Rome as far back as the A.D. 200s. It was carved in a block of marble 43 feet (13 meters) high and 59 feet (18 meters) wide.

- Thanks to satellite weather mapping, scientists can now give much more warning about hazards such as hurricanes. The early warning of Hurricane Katrina in 2005 meant that 80 percent of the people in New Orleans, Louisiana, were evacuated before the storm arrived.

- You can find the town of Argleton, England, on Google Maps, but this town doesn't actually exist. If you went to that location, all you would see are fields. Google says it's a mistake, but some people think it's a joke!

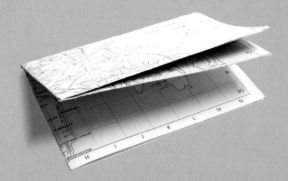

- Vatican City, in Rome, Italy, is the world's smallest independent country. It is called the State of the Vatican City, and it is only 0.17 square miles (0.44 square kilometers) in area.

- Christopher Columbus changed world maps forever when he sailed to the Americas in 1492. But he died believing that he'd actually reached Asia.

- Some cartographers deliberately make small errors on their maps. This is so that they can tell if any other people have copied them instead of making their own maps.

- Satellites can now be used to make maps. Some satellites look at crops. Scientists can tell what crop is being grown on an area as small as one acre.

- The youngest country in the world is Montenegro in southeast Europe. It was formed in 2006.

- You can't make a map of the seabed just by looking at it. This is because even bright sunlight reaches only 1,300 feet (400 meters) under the sea. Below that depth it is completely dark.

- The compass was invented in ancient China, but it wasn't used for navigation at first. Instead, it was used to design and decorate houses according to rules of feng shui. Feng shui is a system of arranging rooms using the directions of north, south, east, and west.

- The earliest known maps are not actually of Earth. On the walls of the Lascaux caves in France, a series of dots shows the stars in the night sky. This map of the heavens was made in 16,500 B.C.

Maps and mapping quiz

The answers to these questions can all be found by looking back through the book. See how many you get right. You can check your answers on page 56.

1) What do scale bars on maps tell us?
   A—temperature
   B—distance
   C—height

2) What do small-scale maps show?
   A—large areas
   B—small areas
   C—temperature

3) What is the capital of Portugal?
   A—Lisbon
   B—Spain
   C—Paris

4) If a compass arrow is pointing straight ahead of you, which way are you facing?
   A—west
   B—south
   C—north

5) The way we show the round Earth on a flat map is called a . . .
   A—reflection
   B—projection
   C—collection

6) What does it mean if contour lines are close together?
   A—the land slopes steeply
   B—the land slopes gently
   C—the land is flat

7) What do you call someone who makes maps?
   A—a photographer
   B—a mapographer
   C—a cartographer

8) Where do you look on a map to find out what a symbol means?
   A—the key
   B—the lock
   C—the scale

9) Which line is at 0 degrees longitude?
   A—the principal meridian
   B—the main meridian
   C—the prime meridian

10) What does a sextant tell you?
    A—how high up in the air you are
    B—how far from the equator you are
    C—how deep the ocean is

11) What is the name given to underwater mountain ranges?
    A—ocean hills
    B—ocean ridges
    C—ocean peaks

12) What instrument do astronomers use to study the stars?
    A—microscope
    B—sextant
    C—telescope

Find out more

Books to read

Map Mania: Discovering Where You Are and Getting to Where You Aren't by Michael A. DiSpezio, Sterling, 2003

Maps and Mapping Skills: Introducing Maps by Meg Gillett, Hodder Wayland, 2008

Maps and Mapping Skills: Understanding Local Maps by Meg Gillett, Hodder Wayland, 2010

Maps and Mapping Skills: Understanding World Maps by Meg Gillett, Hodder Wayland, 2008

The Once Upon a Time Map Book by B. G. Hennessy, Candlewick, 2010

Places to visit

Louisiana State Museum, New Orleans, Louisiana
http://lsm.crt.state.la.us/collections/hcenter.htm
Explore more than 1,400 maps from 1525 to the present, including early periods of exploration and settlement and the early colonies, plus the Civil War and the Battle of New Orleans.

Georgia Museum of Surveying and Mapping, Warrenton, Georgia
www.gamosam.org/index.html
Learn about surveying and mapping by viewing historical tools of the trade, with a specific emphasis on Georgia and surrounding states. Tours are by appointment.

Websites

www.yourchildlearns.com/map-puzzles.htm
Put your knowledge to the test with map puzzles of the United States and the world.

http://kids.nationalgeographic.com/Games/GeographyGames
The *National Geographic* website has lots of great geography quiz games.

www.oxfam.org.uk/education/resources/mapping_our_world
Check out Oxfam's award-winning resource "Mapping Our World," where you can learn all about mapmaking.

http://digitalgallery.nypl.org/nypldigital/dgdivisionbrowseresult.cfm?trg=1&div_id=hm
The New York Public Library's online gallery of map images lets you view historical atlases and maps of the United States and other parts of the world, as well as oceanic charts.

www.maps.google.com
Zoom in on any place on Earth or take a virtual stroll through the streets of some of the world's big cities!

Maps and mapping
quiz answers

1) B	7) C
2) A	8) A
3) A	9) C
4) C	10) B
5) B	11) B
6) A	12) C